W9-BFE-385

VIRGINIA
The Old Dominion State

★

TEN TOP FACTS ABOUT VIRGINIA

★ ★ ★ ★ ★ ★ ★ ★ ★ ★ ★ ★ ★

•State nicknames:	The Old Dominion State, Mother of Presidents
•State motto:	*Sic Semper Tyrannis* (Thus Always to Tyrants)
•Capital:	Richmond
•Area:	40,598 square miles
•State flower:	Dogwood flower
•State tree:	Dogwood
•State bird:	Cardinal
•State dog:	Foxhound
•State fish:	Brook trout
•State shell:	Oyster

To Dan

Photo credits:

p. 4: U.S. Mint; p. 5: (top left) North Wind Picture Archives, Alfred, ME; p. 6: (all) North Wind Picture Archives; p. 7: (right) Brown Brothers, Sterling, PA; p. 8: Superstock Images, Jacksonville, FL; p. 9: (top) North Wind Picture Archives, (bottom right) Brown Brothers; p. 10: North Wind Picture Archives; p. 11: (Portrait of Peyton Randolph) Corbis, (all others) North Wind Picture Archives; p. 13: North Wind Picture Archives; p. 14: (both) North Wind Picture Archives; p. 15: Library of Congress; p. 16: (both) Superstock Images; p. 17: Virginia Tourism Corporation; p. 18: (all) Brown Brothers; p. 19: (top left) Alexandria Black History Resource Center, Alexandria, VA, (bottom left) G.E. Kidder Smith/Corbis, (right) Superstock Images; p. 20: (top left) D. Muench, (top right) Superstock Images; p. 21: (top left) Virginia Tourism Corporation, (top right) N. Carter/North Wind Picture Archives, (bottom right) Virginia Tourism Corporation; p. 22: (left) Superstock Images, Bettmann/Corbis, New York, NY (Ashe), Brown Brothers (Bailey); p. 23 Mitch Gerbis/Corbis (Beatty), Superstock Images (Cather), MGM/Verve Records (Fitzgerald), Superstock Images (Henry); p. 24: North Wind Picture Archives (Lee, Lewis and Clark), Bettmann/Corbis (Robinson, Snead); p. 25: North Wind Picture Archives.

Photo research by Dwayne Howard

All other illustrations by John Speirs

No part of this publication may be reproduced in whole or in part, or stored in a retrieval system, or transmitted in any form or by any means, electronic, mechanical, photocopying, recording, or otherwise, without written permission of the publisher. For information regarding permission, write to Scholastic Inc., Attention: Permissions Department, 555 Broadway, New York, NY 10012.

ISBN 0-439-22297-4

Copyright © 2001 by Scholastic Inc.

Published by Scholastic Inc. SCHOLASTIC and associated logos are trademarks and/or registered trademarks of Scholastic Inc. All rights reserved.

The Official 50 State Quarters Club is a publication of Scholastic Inc. that has been developed in conjunction with The Jim Henson Company under a license from the United States Mint. 50 State Quarters, the 50 State Quarters logo, and the official Treasury Department/United States Mint seal are trademarks of the United States Mint. JIM HENSON is a trademark of The Jim Henson Company. All rights reserved.

THE
Jim Henson
—COMPANY—

12 11 10 9 8 7 6 5 4 3 2 1   1 2 3 4 5/0

Designed by Madalina Stefan

Printed in the U.S.A.

First Scholastic printing, June 2001

Scholastic has a wide range of fun, high-quality book clubs for children of all ages. Please visit our Web site at www.scholastic.com/athomeclubs.

VIRGINIA
The Old Dominion State

By Kristin Pederson

SCHOLASTIC INC.

New York   Toronto   London   Auckland   Sydney   Mexico City   New Delhi   Hong Kong

A Celebration of the Fifty States

★ ★ ★ ★ ★ ★ ★ ★ ★ ★ ★ ★

In January 1999, the U.S. Mint started an ambitious ten-year program to commemorate each of the fifty United States. Over the next several years (through 2008), they will issue five newly designed quarters each year.

One side (obverse) of each new quarter will display the profile of George Washington and the words *Liberty, In God We Trust,* and *United States of America.* The other side (reverse) will feature a design honoring a specific state's unique history, the year it became a state, the year of the quarter's issue, and the words *E Pluribus Unum* (Latin for "from many, one"). The quarters are being issued in the order in which the states joined the Union, beginning with the thirteen original colonies.

To find out more about the 50 State Quarters™ Program, visit the official U.S. Mint Web site at *www.USMINT.gov.*

VIRGINIA'S QUARTER: Three Brave Ships

Imagine leaving behind your family, your friends, your home, and crowding onto a tiny ship. Imagine the freezing-cold wind biting at your fingers as you wave good-bye to everything you have ever known. Now imagine not knowing exactly where you are headed, how long you will be at sea, or what your destination will be like when you arrive, *if* you arrive.

This was the experience of 140 adventurous English men and boys during the chilly London winter of 1606. The British king, James I, sent three ships to the New World, hoping to discover riches and expand the British Empire. After four grueling months crossing the ocean, the *Susan Constant, Godspeed,* and *Discovery* landed about sixty miles south of Chesapeake Bay. On those shores, the English built Jamestown, our nation's first British settlement.

Jamestown, named for King James I, will turn four hundred years old in 2007. In honor of this anniversary, Virginia's quarter depicts the three historic ships that crossed the ocean in 1606. These ships, replicas of which are moored in Jamestown's harbor, remind us of the perseverance and sense of adventure held by Virginia's founders. They tell a story of Virginia's people not only surviving, but thriving during challenging times.

Map of the Jamestown settlement

In the Beginning

Long before the first Europeans even knew about the New World, Native American tribes lived in the land we now call Virginia. The region's lush coastal forests and riverbanks belonged to a proud tribe called the Powhatan. To the west, in the Shenandoah Valley, the Sioux Indians hunted buffalo and farmed the rich land.

Native Americans hunting buffalo

The landing of the *Susan Constant, Godspeed,* and *Discovery*

In 1607, Virginia's native inhabitants were joined by "new neighbors." The passengers on the three ships depicted on Virginia's quarter left England for the New World hoping to achieve four goals. Backed by England's new Virginia Company, they wanted to scout out a sea passage to Asia, find the area's richest natural resources, convert the natives to the Anglican religion, and bring glory to England.

Despite these high hopes, the settlers' journey seemed cursed. The men were hungry, sick, and discouraged. Many lives were lost. After a four-month voyage, on April 27, 1607, 105 of the 140 members of the original group finally reached the shores of Cape Henry, at the mouth of the Chesapeake Bay.

Their struggles, however, were just beginning. Upon arrival, the Englishmen were attacked by Native Americans. They fled to their ships and headed upriver, searching for a more protected site. On May 13, 1607, the weary group finally dropped anchor nine miles southwest of what is now Williamsburg. They named their new home Jamestown and established the first permanent English settlement in the New World.

Colonists settling Jamestown

In 1608, Captain John Smith was chosen as president of the settlement. Smith was thought of by many as a vain, harsh tyrant. Nevertheless, he was a strong leader, which is exactly what the struggling colony needed. Under Smith's guidance, the colonists made Jamestown into a small English-style town. They built a fort, planted crops, and searched for gold. However, the settlers were not prepared for this harsh new wilderness. Malnutrition and typhoid abounded and many of them died.

Captain John Smith

Lord De La Warr

Despite these problems, Smith's strict leadership helped the settlement grow. He organized trade with the native people and led expeditions to explore and map the area. On one such adventure, Smith was captured by the powerful Native American chief Powhatan. Legend has it

Chief Powhatan

that Smith was saved by the chief's daughter, Pocahontas, although many historians consider this dramatic story folklore.

In 1609, Smith was horribly burned in a gunpowder accident and had to return to England for treatment. A new charter was granted, and Thomas West, also known as Lord De La Warr, was appointed governor. A man named Sir Thomas Gates was appointed deputy governor and was sent ahead to the settlement with a fleet of ships carrying fresh supplies. Unfortunately, Gates and his men encountered a fierce hurricane in the West Indies. After four frightening days of drifting through perilous waters, the lead ship, the *Sea Venture,* finally became wedged on a reef off Bermuda. Miraculously, all 150 people aboard survived. Even the supplies were undamaged. The colonists began building two new boats from the wreckage.

These two ships, the *Deliverance* and the *Patience,* finally arrived in Jamestown to find fierce warring, sickness, and chaos. The

Tobacco plant

flavor. A settler named John Rolfe introduced a type of West Indian tobacco to the area that flourished in Virginia's fertile soil, becoming Jamestown's main crop. This tobacco was in great demand in England in 1614 when Virginians began shipping the plentiful plants there. During that year, Rolfe also married Pocahontas, saying that their union was "for the good of this plantation, and the honor of our countrie." Their union did indeed help the Powhatan and settlers get along for a short time. With this temporary peace and Rolfe's profitable tobacco, Jamestown thrived.

Powhatan had imprisoned the settlers in their own fortress. This winter of 1609 – 1610 is known as the "starving time." Only sixty people survived. In June 1610, Jamestown's discouraged citizens gave up and abandoned the settlement.

When word of the settlers' decision to leave Jamestown reached King James, he was not happy. Lord De La Warr, the settlement's new governor, set sail for the colony. Some say Lord De La Warr's well-stocked ships actually met the colonists' departing boat, and the king's new leader ordered them to turn around! In any case, the ships returned to Jamestown to start over.

During this time of rebuilding, the settlers "struck gold" in the form of a sweet-smelling leaf. The Native Americans had shown them how to plant tobacco; however, the leaves had too strong and bitter a

Marriage of Pocahontas and John Rolfe

This was a prosperous time for the settlement. The first Africans arrived in Jamestown in 1619 to supply the working hands the settlement desperately needed. These Africans were cruelly kidnapped from their native countries. However, unlike the Africans who were later kidnapped and brought to America as slaves, these first Africans were allowed to work as indentured servants. This meant that after seven years of service, they could own their own property and live as free people.

Pocahontas

Who Was the Real Pocahontas?

Pocahontas's real name was Matoaka, and she was the daughter of Chief Powhatan, the powerful leader of approximately thirty tribes in the Chesapeake Bay and Tidewater area of Virginia. Her nickname, "Pocahontas," means "playful child."

Pocahontas is generally thought of as a young woman who worked to create peace between her Native American community and the Jamestown colonists. However, many conflicting stories surround the spirited girl. The most famous legend says that she saved Jamestown colonist John Smith from being killed by her father in 1607. At this time, she would have been about ten or eleven years old.

Some scholars point out that the first time John Smith mentioned this near-execution was seventeen years after it happened, and he could have invented it. In fact, in an account Smith wrote right after his winter stay with Chief Powhatan's people, he never noted the dramatic event. Smith instead reported that he had been kept comfortable and was treated in a friendly way by Chief Powhatan's people. The story is now considered folklore for this reason.

Another story about Pocahontas involves her marriage to John Rolfe, the colonist who brought West Indian tobacco to the New World. In 1612, Pocahontas was taken prisoner by the English. She was held hostage at Jamestown for over a year. During this time, she met the twenty-eight-year-old Rolfe. Some accounts say the two fell in love and married. Others say that as a condition of her release, Pocahontas agreed to marry Rolfe. Regardless, in April 1614, Pocahontas and Rolfe wed. She changed her name to Rebecca Rolfe, and the couple had a son named Thomas Rolfe.

In the spring of 1616, Rolfe took his wife to England. Some scholars describe this trip as a wonderful visit to the land whose leaders had called her father, Chief Powhatan, the emperor of Virginia. Other historians say that the Virginia Company of London, which was in charge of establishing Jamestown, used Rebecca to promote the colony to English people. By all accounts, Rebecca attended fancy parties, went to the theater, and enjoyed fine restaurants. Just before she was to return to Virginia, she fell ill with smallpox. She died on March 21, 1617, in Gravesend, England, at the young age of 21.

Virginians defending themselves against Native Americans

Rumblings of Revolution

By the early 1620s, Jamestown faced new hurdles. After the short truce created by Rolfe and Pocahontas's marriage, Chief Powhatan's people began to realize that these strangers from across the ocean not only intended to stay, but planned to bring more settlers from their homeland. This realization so alarmed the natives that, in 1622, they launched an attack that killed four hundred settlers. Due to Native American warring and devastating sickness, the settlers' population was shrinking. In 1624, the king took over for the Virginia Company in governing the colonists and Jamestown became the first royal colony.

By this time, King James I had appointed Sir William Berkeley as the colony's governor. Despite the loss of English lives in Jamestown, the colonists still numbered 5,000. These people lived mostly along the James and York Rivers, the eastern shore, and the Hampton Roads area. Many worked as farmers, artisans, and tradesmen. Some worked as "watermen," or fishermen, netting crabs and many

Sir William Berkeley

9

kinds of fish off Virginia's coast and in its tidal rivers.

In 1644, all was not well in the settlers' homeland. British King Charles I's ideas about the supremacy of the Anglican religion had sparked a civil war. On January 27, 1649, Charles I was sentenced to death as a tyrant and enemy of the nation, and was beheaded at Whitehall, London. Many of his supporters fled to the New World and refused to recognize the new British government led by Oliver Cromwell. These Englishmen established a gentry or "uppercrust" society that remained loyal to the monarchy. In 1660, when King Charles II took the throne, he is said to have called Virginia "Old Dominion" due to its constant loyalty to the throne. The king's colonial policies, however, soon began to cause unrest among the settlers. Tobacco sales were strongly controlled by London merchants, making it hard for the Virginia farmers to turn a profit. This restricted trade, along with lack of royal support for defending against Native American attacks, angered the colonists.

Governor Berkeley largely ignored the colonists' continued plight with the Native Americans. Against the governor's wishes, a colonist named Nathaniel Bacon decided to take matters into his own hands by organizing a militia and attacking a Powhatan village in 1676. Governor Berkeley was furious at Bacon for disobeying his commands. He called Bacon a traitor, and Bacon's Rebellion began. The rebel force occupied Jamestown, drove out the governor, and launched another attack against the Native Americans.

Bacon's Rebellion

Governor Berkeley, however, soon regained control. Although Bacon was unsuccessful, his rebellion marked the beginning of the colonists' struggle against English rule.

By 1707, when Virginia celebrated its one hundredth birthday, the tobacco industry was booming. However, the profits were controlled by just a handful of English estate owners. The demands of farming tobacco also increased the need for extra labor. In order to fill this need, Africans were shipped to the New World to work as slaves.

In 1765, the colonists, already furious about their tobacco profits being withheld, grew even angrier when England imposed several new taxes. During the next decade, Virginia moved steadily toward revolution.

Virginia Fights for Freedom

Virginia played an important role in the Revolutionary War and the events leading up to it. Colonial leaders met at the first Continental Congress, held in Philadelphia in 1774, to discuss their problems with England. Virginia furnished the Continental Congress's first president, Peyton Randolph. By the time the Second Continental Congress met less than a year later, the American Revolution had already begun.

The Congress appointed a young Virginian named George Washington, who had been a hero in the French and Indian War, to lead the colonial forces. While Washington guided the Continental

Peyton Randolph   Thomas Jefferson writing the Declaration of Independence

army, another young Virginian named Thomas Jefferson was asked to write an explanation of the colonists' position for Britain's King George. This document, which was signed by delegates from all thirteen colonies, became the Declaration of Independence. It stated that all men are created equal and that the colonists should be granted the rights of "Life, Liberty, and the Pursuit of Happiness."

During the first six years of the Revolution, Virginia's capital was moved from Williamsburg, where it had been located since 1700, to Richmond. In 1781, led by the infamous traitor Benedict Arnold, the British invaded Richmond, and then occupied the port town of Yorktown. General Washington advanced his army to Yorktown and forced the outnumbered British to surrender. Although battles continued in New York for another eighteen months, the surrender in Yorktown marked the end of the American Revolution.

General George Washington leading the Continental army

11

Peace, Philadelphia, and Presidents

For the first decade following the war, the thirteen colonies largely operated independently of one another. The colonies' leaders soon recognized a need for solidarity. A committee was formed, including Virginians George Washington and James Madison, to draft the United States Constitution in 1787. In 1788, Virginia became the nation's tenth state when its representatives ratified the Constitution.

The beginning of the nineteenth century was a prosperous time for some Virginians. Though plantation owners made huge profits on cotton and tobacco crops worked by slaves, most small farm families struggled to raise peanuts, potatoes, corn, hogs, chickens, and cattle on less than four hundred acres.

As the century wore on, even the most wealthy and privileged Virginians experienced tough times. The many decades of tobacco farming had exhausted the soil. Farmers found it increasingly difficult to produce the treasured crop and had to seek other ways to support themselves. Abandoning their farms, many people moved to western Virginia to mine coal, salt, and ore.

This change in Virginia's economy also raised the question of slavery. Many Virginians thought slavery was the perfect solution to their labor needs; other citizens understood that slavery was evil and immoral. By the middle of the nineteenth century, change was in the air.

Coal mine

Nat Turner's Revolution

Not all Virginians enjoyed freedom after the American Revolution. Born in 1800, slave Nat Turner belonged to a small plantation owner in rural Southampton County, Virginia. He learned to read from one of his master's sons and enjoyed the religious training he received on the plantation. As a young man, Turner believed he was chosen by God to lead his people out of bondage. He eventually led the most famous slave rebellion in American history.

Nat Turner was sold to a neighboring farmer in the 1820s and was sold again in 1831 to a craftsman named Joseph Travis. While he was working on the Travis estate, Turner received what he considered to be a sign from God (the occurrence of a solar eclipse) that the time had come for him to lead an uprising.

On the night of August 21, 1831, together with twelve other slaves, Nat Turner began his violent revolt. He murdered Travis and his family and then marched toward the county seat of Jerusalem, Virginia. Within two days and nights,

Soldier capturing Nat Turner

The Civil War: Slavery and Secession

In 1832, a year after Turner's uprising in Southampton, state leaders drew up a plan for gradual emancipation (freeing of slaves) in an attempt to address the ongoing problem of slavery. However, the plan did not pass in the Virginia Assembly. The slavery issue continued to burn until Abraham Lincoln was elected President.

When President Lincoln finally called for an end to slavery in 1860, seven Southern "cotton" states quickly seceded, or broke away, from the Union. At first, Virginia remained in the Union. However, when Lincoln asked Virginia to fight with the North against slavery, Old Dominion followed her sister states and seceded in 1861.

During the Civil War, Richmond became the capital of the Confederacy, and over half of the Civil War battles took place in the state. The war's first major clash and the signing of its final peace treaty both occurred in Virginia. Native son Robert E. Lee was chosen to lead the Confederate forces.

The First Battle of Bull Run, also called the Battle of Manassas, occurred on July 21, 1861. Both sides wore blue and gray uniforms, so the Confederate and Union soldiers had difficulty telling friend from enemy. Because the early Confederate flag looked so much like the Stars and Stripes, some gunners actually fired on their own troops.

Although the Union soldiers won this initial fight, Virginian leader General

Turner and his small army of slaves killed about sixty white people.

Turner's revolution was doomed from the start. There was a lack of discipline among his followers, and only about seventy-five slaves ended up joining his cause, whereas the townspeople and the militia, who were prepared to fight Turner's forces, numbered 3,000 men. Turner's tiny group of rebels was defeated. In the hysteria that followed the uprising, many innocent slaves were murdered. When Turner was captured, he was tried and hanged.

Before those two nightmarish days in 1831, many white Southerners believed that blacks were happy being slaves. Nat Turner's revolution put an end to that myth. He had dreamed of freedom for all African-Americans; however, his revolution had the opposite effect. After the revolt, the education of slaves was prohibited. African-Americans were not permitted to assemble in groups or travel. Proslavery feelings were strengthened. These conditions persisted until (and throughout) the Civil War.

Battle of Bull Run

Thomas Jonathan Jackson later led his men to victory in other battles in the state. Jackson's soldiers were so strong that the Virginia Brigade was compared to a "stone wall," and Jackson carried the nickname of "Stonewall" until his death.

In June 1862, Union soldiers fought their way up the peninsula toward Richmond. General Robert E. Lee defended the capital in a series of battles that left many dead on both sides. Finally, on April 1, 1865, Union forces crushed the weakened Confederate army, capturing the

General Robert E. Lee

town of Petersburg and then Richmond itself. On April 9, 1865, General Lee surrendered at the Appomattox Courthouse. The Civil War was over, leaving 700,000 Americans dead.

Rebuilding and Rebounding

After the Civil War, Virginia was in ruins. Farms were destroyed, thousands were dead, and poverty plagued the state. People turned to sharecropping — farmers rented and worked other farmers' land in return for a share of the profits, but both the tenants and landowners were often in debt. New industries, such as textile mills and cigarette factories, sprang up and helped the state recover from the war. Newly built railroad lines carried products from the West to the eastern seaports for export. Shipbuilding boomed in the town of Newport News, still one of the nation's largest shipyards. Coal mines in southwest Virginia employed many people, and thousands found work in Chesapeake Bay fisheries and in seafood processing plants.

View of destroyed region of Richmond after the Civil War

Virginia at Midcentury

At the turn of the century, though, poverty was still widespread in the state.

When the country entered World War I in 1917, the state's factories and munitions plants produced supplies for America's soldiers, bringing prosperity to Virginians. Military training camps also multiplied throughout the state, creating yet another industry that helped Virginia in the dark days of the Great Depression of the 1930s.

In the period before the United States entered World War II, the first state defense system was established in Virginia. The war brought thousands of soldiers into Virginia's military camps, and the expansion of the Norfolk naval base and the shipyards in Newport News brought prosperity. Virginia was finally on the upswing.

Not every Virginian shared in the prosperous times of the early twentieth century. The state enacted Jim Crow laws, laws that called for the separation of blacks and whites. Segregation led to separate schools, separate stores, and even separate drinking fountains for both black and white people.

In 1954, the Supreme Court ruled that segregation in schools was illegal. Harry F. Byrd, a senator from Virginia, began a campaign called the Massive Resistance to keep segregation legal. Many schools around the state followed this doctrine, and one entire school district actually closed all of its public schools just to avoid integration. Finally, in the late fifties, Virginia began complying with the law.

Virginia Today

Almost four hundred years after its shaky beginnings, Virginia is thriving. Virginians no longer rely quite as heavily on farming as their ancestors did. However, tobacco and other crops still bring wealth to the state. Bountiful apple orchards dot the Shenandoah Valley, and Tidewater County farmers produce Virginia's famous Smithfield hams.

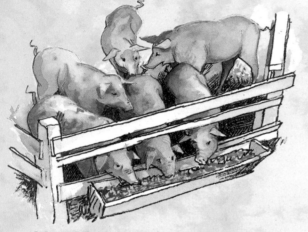

Many Virginians also work in the manufacturing and government sectors. Telecommunications equipment, chemicals, furniture, printed materials, railroad equipment, and processed foods are all produced in the state.

"Watermen" still have their place in Virginia. Fisheries furnish jobs for 6,000 to 10,000 citizens. One-third of the blue crabs in America are caught in Virginia. The coastal counties play host to seafood plants and factories that create fertilizer from fishing byproducts. Finally, shipbuilding remains both a beloved craft and a moneymaker for the state.

Thanks to statewide preservation efforts, much of Virginia is still as beautiful today as it was when Chief Powhatan

Virginia Beach

ruled the region. Each year, thousands of hikers, bikers, bird-watchers, beachcombers, and folks who like to sink a fishing line and spend a lazy afternoon angling all find what they are looking for in Virginia. Shenandoah National Park, along the crest of the Blue Ridge Mountains, hosts nearly two million visitors a year. Sand and surf seekers venture to beautiful Virginia Beach and Back Bay National Wildlife Refuge. Even in Virginia's urban areas, natural beauty is close at hand. The Washington and Old Dominion Trail begins in metropolitan Arlington, and features scenic views of the Blue Ridge Mountains.

Blue Ridge Mountains

Shenandoah Valley

Virginia: Land of Leaders

George Washington

Thomas Jefferson

James Madison

James Monroe

Another nickname for Virginia is "Mother of Presidents," and that is no exaggeration. Four of the first five Presidents called Virginia home, and the state has contributed eight Presidents in all. In fact, Virginian Presidents served for more than two consecutive decades, from 1801 to 1825. Here are some facts about Virginia's presidential powerhouses.

George Washington (1732 – 1799) was the first President of the United States. He served from 1789 to 1797. Nicknamed the "Father of His Country," Washington had no formal education. He worked as a planter, surveyor, and a soldier before becoming President on the Federalist Party ticket. Although many people encouraged Washington to seek a third term, he was tired of politics and refused.

Thomas Jefferson (1743 – 1826) was the third President of the United States. He served from 1801 to 1809. Jefferson had many nicknames. He was called "Man of the People" for his commitment to justice and his authorship of the Declaration of Independence. A skilled jack-of-all-trades, he was also a philosopher and architect. In fact, although he had no architectural training, he designed and erected many of the buildings at the University of Virginia. He also created Monticello, his majestic home in Charlottesville. His wisdom and success in so many areas earned Jefferson the title of the "Sage of Monticello."

James Madison (1751 – 1836) was the fourth President of the United States. He served from 1809 to 1817, and was nicknamed "Father of the Constitution." Madison graduated from the College of New Jersey (now Princeton University) in 1771 and worked as a lawyer before becoming President on the Democratic–Republican party ticket. He played a large role in writing Virginia's state constitution in 1776. However, when Madison was called the "Father of the Constitution," he argued that the document was not "the offspring of a single brain," but "the work of many heads and many hands."

James Monroe (1758 – 1831) was the fifth President of the United States. He served from 1817 to 1825. Monroe graduated from the College of William and Mary (the second-oldest institution of higher learning in the country after Harvard) in 1776 and worked as a lawyer. Thomas Jefferson once said, "Monroe was so honest that if you turned his soul inside out there would not be a spot on it."

Other Presidents born in Virginia are William Henry Harrison (1773 – 1841), the ninth President, who died in 1841 after just one month in office; John Tyler (1790 – 1862), the tenth President, who served from 1841 to 1845; Zachary Taylor (1784 – 1850), the twelfth President, who served from 1849 to 1850; and Woodrow Wilson (1856 – 1924), the twenty-eighth President, who served from 1913 to 1921.

Things to Do and Places to See

The African-American Heritage Park

This Alexandria attraction offers a combination of history, nature, and beauty. Of twenty-one known slave burials on this site, six headstones remain in their original location. Visitors can learn about African-Americans' contributions to Alexandria as they stroll through preserved areas, where mallards, painted turtles, beavers, and crayfish live in their natural habitat. Sculptures throughout the park also honor important African-Americans and their accomplishments.

Belle Grove

Belle Grove Plantation

Walk into the eighteenth century as you tour this grand home, located on one hun-dred acres in Middleton. This site served as Union General Philip Henry Sheridan's headquarters before and after the Battle of Cedar Creek in October 1864. The home is filled with traditional blue-and-white porcelain, pewter, old-fashioned wooden toys, hand-thrown pottery, gardening tools, needlework, quilting fabrics, and handwoven rugs from old Virginia. Visitors can also learn the dramatic history of the Shenandoah Valley during the Civil War era.

Roller coaster at Busch Gardens

Busch Gardens

This theme park is designed to look and feel like a small European vil-lage. Visitors can enjoy shows, music, and rides. Busch Gardens boasts the Alpengeist, which is the world's tallest, fastest, twisting roller coaster. For those who like calmer entertainment, the park offers specialty foods from Germany, France, and Italy. Nature lovers can visit Jack Hanna's Wild Reserve, where hun-dreds of birds and animals live in their natural habitats.

Victory monument in Yorktown

Colonial National Historical Park

This Yorktown attraction is the site of the last major battle of the American Revolution. On these grounds in 1781, General George Washington's soldiers, assisted by French troops, defeated the British and won America's independence. The Yorktown Visitor Center features a museum and a short film about the battle. Venture out on a ranger-guided tour, which highlights the battlefield and eighteenth-century town, or experience a driving tour through the battlefield sites.

False Cape State Park

This area earned its name because its land mass looked so much like Cape Henry that sailors were accidentally lured into its shallow waters. Today, it is no longer a dead-end for ships, but a launching pad for fun. Visitors can hike through the quiet maritime forests and explore the sandy dunes that line the Atlantic Ocean. This Virginia preserve is only accessible by boat, bike, or foot, so it is the perfect peaceful, rustic getaway for dedicated campers.

Mount Vernon

Mount Vernon Estates and Gardens

George Washington's historic home in Mount Vernon, a mansion with rooms painted the same bright colors it was in colonial times, is filled with original furniture, pictures, and heirlooms. Visit more than a dozen restored outbuildings, including the greenhouse, stables, slave quarters, and kitchen, and tour the museum exhibitions. The grounds also feature a Slave Memorial and Burial Ground, Washington's Tomb, active archaeological digs, as well as beautiful gardens and nature trails to explore.

Pamplin Historical Park and The National Museum of the Civil War Soldier

Opened in 1994, this Petersburg attraction has been called "the new crown jewel of Civil War history destinations in America." The 422-acre park features world-class museums, an antebellum plantation home, and

Musket firing demonstration,
National Museum of the Civil War Soldier

Cliff in the Blue Ridge Mountains,
Shenandoah National Park

living history demonstrations. Visitors can see the historic battlefield where, on April 2, 1865, Union forces broke through Petersburg's defense lines. This event resulted in the capture of the Confederate capital city of Richmond and General Robert E. Lee's surrender.

Pamunkey Indian Museum

Located on the Pamunkey Indian Reservation, this museum show-cases the history, traditions, and beliefs of the Pamunkey Nation (another name for Powhatan), from the Ice Age to today. Visitors can also watch the Pamunkey women create the tribe's noted pottery. Modern-day tribal members use the same tools and methods their ancestors invented centuries ago.

Shenandoah National Park

The Native American word *Shenandoah* means "Daughter of the Stars." Tip your head toward the dazzling night sky at this national park,

and you will discover why the Powhatan chose this beautiful name for the region. The Shenandoah National Park features natural wonders ranging from caverns to waterfalls to mountain peaks. Visitors can tour the park's centuries-old towns, hop on horses and explore breathtaking trails, or take a canoe, kayak, or inner tube down the river.

Aquarium at the Virginia Marine Science Museum

Virginia Marine Science Museum

At this interactive science museum, you can make your own hurricane and dig for oysters. Featuring more than 100,000 aquariums, the museum takes visitors on a journey of the state's waters. See the indoor Coastal River Room, where birds and turtles actually roam free. Marvel at the 50,000-gallon aquarium that features the world's largest collection of Chesapeake Bay fish. Touch gentle stingrays, horseshoe crabs, and other marine life. The museum also offers seasonal boat trips for dolphin and whale watching.

Governor's Palace, Colonial Williamsburg

Williamsburg

A British flag flies overhead. People stroll the cobblestone streets in high-button shoes and old-fashioned English suits. Bangers and mash (sausage and potatoes) are served at the local tavern. Although these surroundings suggest colonial times, this is actually a description of modern Williamsburg. This town lets tourists experience time travel with its historic buildings, costumed actors, guided tours, and demonstrations of crafts and handiwork from the period. The Historic Area, where the past comes alive with militia drills, public oration in the style of Patrick Henry, and other recreations, hosts over one million visitors a year.

Famous People from Virginia

Arthur Ashe (1943 – 1993)

Tennis player Arthur Ashe wowed the world by being the first African-American man to win a major tennis tournament, the United States Open, in 1968. After that, Ashe went on to win three major world tournaments — the Australian Open, the French Open, and Wimbledon.

Pearl Bailey (1918 – 1990)

This popular nightclub singer starred in the first all African-American version of *Hello, Dolly!* in 1967. She also appeared in numerous films, plays, and television programs. Bailey also served as the United States Goodwill Ambassador to the United Nations, and worked to fight AIDS, illiteracy, and child abuse.

Warren Beatty (1938 –)

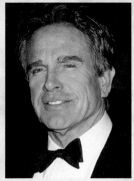

Henry Warren Beatty grew up in Richmond and went on to become one of America's premier actors, directors, and filmmakers. His film credits include *Bonnie and Clyde, Shampoo, Reds,* and *Heaven Can Wait.* He has received numerous Academy Awards nominations and won an Oscar for Best Director in 1981. Beatty has also received several Golden Globe Awards. He is the younger brother of actress Shirley MacLaine, who was also born in Richmond.

Ella Fitzgerald (1917 – 1996)

One of the leading jazz singers of all time, Ella Fitzgerald grew up in the town of Newport News. Her career began at Amateur Night at Harlem's Apollo Theater, and she went on to work with jazz legends such as Louis Armstrong, Duke Ellington, Benny Goodman, and Dizzy Gillespie. Fitzgerald's trademark singing style, called scat, featured nonsense syllables invented to imitate the sounds of musical instruments.

Willa Cather (1873 – 1947)

Writer Willa Cather's novels, such as *O Pioneers!* and *My Antonia,* paint pictures of rural American life in the late nineteenth century and depict strong, determined female characters. Born near Winchester, Cather moved with her family to Red Cloud, Nebraska, when she was ten years old. In addition to being a novelist, Cather worked as an editor, teacher, newspaper writer, and poet. She won a Pulitzer Prize in 1923 for her novel *One of Ours.*

Patrick Henry (1736 – 1799)

Lawyer and patriot Patrick Henry was a living symbol of the American struggle for liberty and democracy. As early as 1763, Henry began speaking out against British rule at his law practice in Hanover County. He bluntly criticized the British for enacting the Stamp Act in 1765, and became a leader in the movement for colonial rights. He is most famous for saying, "I know not what course others may take; but as for me, give me liberty or give me death." Patrick Henry served three terms as governor of Virginia.

Robert E. Lee (1807 – 1870)

Robert E. Lee, general of the Confederate army during the Civil War, was born on a plantation called Stratford in Westmoreland County. Lee later attended West Point, where he was at the top of his class. He led many famous battles during the war, including those at Gettysburg and Appomattax. Lee surrendered to Union general Ulysses S. Grant at the Appomattax Courthouse on April 9, 1865, bringing an end to the Civil War.

Bill "Bojangles" Robinson (1878 – 1949)

Born Luther Robinson, the "King of Tap Dancers" was raised by his grandmother in Richmond. Bojangles (a childhood nickname) eventually became widely known for single-handedly saving failing Broadway shows with his amazing dancing. Robinson could dance anywhere — he once tapped backward for sixty blocks. His most visible role was as Shirley Temple's dancing partner in four films.

Meriwether Lewis (1774 – 1809) and William Clark (1770 – 1838)

These Virginian-born explorers both served as captains in the U.S. infantry and worked for a rifle company prior to taking up exploration. From 1804 to 1806, the pair successfully cocommanded the Corps of Discovery (known as the Lewis and Clark Expedition) on an expedition leading west from St. Louis, Missouri, to the Pacific Ocean. After returning, both men served as governors, Lewis as governor of the Louisiana Territory and Clark as governor of the Missouri Territory.

Sam Snead (1912 –)

Sam Snead, a professional golfer from Ashwood, spent his boyhood days caddying at a local golf club. He won a record eighty-one Professional Golfers' Association (PGA) tour events in his career and took home trophies in the PGA championships, the Masters, and the British Open. Also known as "Slammin' Sammy," Snead was famous for his "sidewinder" putting technique, in which he faced the hole and hit the ball, holding his hand low on the club shaft.

Booker T. Washington: Life Before Freedom

Booker T. Washington (1856 – 1915), one of America's most celebrated educators, was born into slavery near the town of Roanoke. Washington went to school in Franklin County, not as a student, but to carry books for one of his owner's children. It was illegal to educate slaves. "I had the feeling that to get into the schoolhouse and study would be about the same as getting into paradise," he once wrote. After emancipation in 1865, Washington took a job in a salt mine that began at four A.M. so he could attend school during the day. Later he studied at the Hampton Institute in Virginia, where he paid his tuition by doing chores. As an adult, he founded the Tuskegee Institute in Alabama in 1881, one of the first and finest predominantly black universities. The following excerpt from Washington's memoir, An Autobiography: A Story of My Life and Work, *paints a picture of Virginia's early days from a slave's perspective.*

As nearly as I can get at the facts, I was born in the year 1858 or 1859. At the time I came into the world no careful registry of births of people of my complexion was kept. My birthplace was near Hale's Ford, in Franklin County, Virginia. It was about as near to Nowhere as any locality gets to be, so far as I can learn. Hale's Ford, I think, was a town with one house and a post-office, and my birth place was on a large plantation several miles distant from it.

I remember very distinctly the appearance of the cabin in which I was born and lived until freedom came. It was a small log cabin about 12 x 16 feet, and without windows. There was no floor, except one of dirt. There was a large opening in the center of the floor, where sweet potatoes were kept for my master's family during the winter. . . . Our bed, or "pallet," as we called it, was made every night on the dirt floor. Our bed clothing consisted of a few rags gathered here and there.

One thing I remember more vividly than any other in connection with the days when I was a slave was my dress, or, rather, my lack of dress. . . . The only garment that I remember receiving from my owners during the war was a "tow shirt." When I did not wear this shirt I was positively without any garment.

In Virginia, the tow shirt was quite an institution during slavery. This shirt was made of the refuse flax that grew in that part of Virginia, and it was a veritable instrument of torture. It was stiff and coarse. Until it had been worn for about six weeks it made one feel as if a thousand needle points were pricking his flesh. I suppose I was about six years old when I was given one of these shirts to wear. After repeated trials the torture was more than my childish flesh could endure and I gave it up in despair. To this day the sight of a new shirt revives the recollection of the tortures of my first new shirt. In the midst of my despair, in connection with this garment, my brother John, who was about two years older than I, did me a kindness which I shall never forget. He volunteered to wear my new shirt for me until it was "broken in." After he had worn it for several weeks I ventured to wear it myself, but not without pain.

As soon as I was old enough I performed what, to me, was important service, in holding the horses, and riding behind the white women of the household on their long horseback rides, which were very common in those days. At one time, while holding the horses and assisting quite a party of visiting ladies to mount their horses, I remember that, just before the visitors rode away, a tempting plate of ginger cakes was brought out and handed around to the visitors. This, I think, was the first time that I had ever seen any ginger cakes, and a very deep impression was made upon my childish mind. I remember I said to myself that if I ever could get to the point where I could eat ginger cakes as I saw those ladies eating them, the height of my ambition would be reached.

An easy, cheesy snack made with world-famous Virginia ham

Virginia is known for its mouthwatering, honey-cured hams. For a taste of the Old Dominion, roll up a batch of Ham and Cheddar Pinwheels!

You will need:

- 1 package (eight) refrigerated crescent rolls
- mustard
- 1/4 cup shredded cheddar cheese
- 1/4 cup finely chopped, cooked ham (Virginia ham is tastiest, of course.)

Now just follow these simple steps:

- Ask an adult to help you set the oven to 375°F.
- Unroll the crescent rolls. Tear along the perforations.
- Place the triangles on an ungreased baking sheet.
- Spread the triangles lightly with mustard.
- Sprinkle each with 1 tablespoon cheese and 1 tablespoon cooked ham.
- Starting at the large end, roll the dough toward point. Fold each end slightly to form "horns."
- Bake at 375° for 11 to 13 minutes.

Ask an adult to help you remove your pinwheels from the oven. Serve piping hot, with a tall, cold glass of Virginia's state drink, milk!

Makes eight pinwheels.